A
WILD CHILD'S GUIDE TO
NATURE
AT NIGHT

For Tony and Debbie

~ DARA

For Luna, Zoey and Evie

~ BARRY

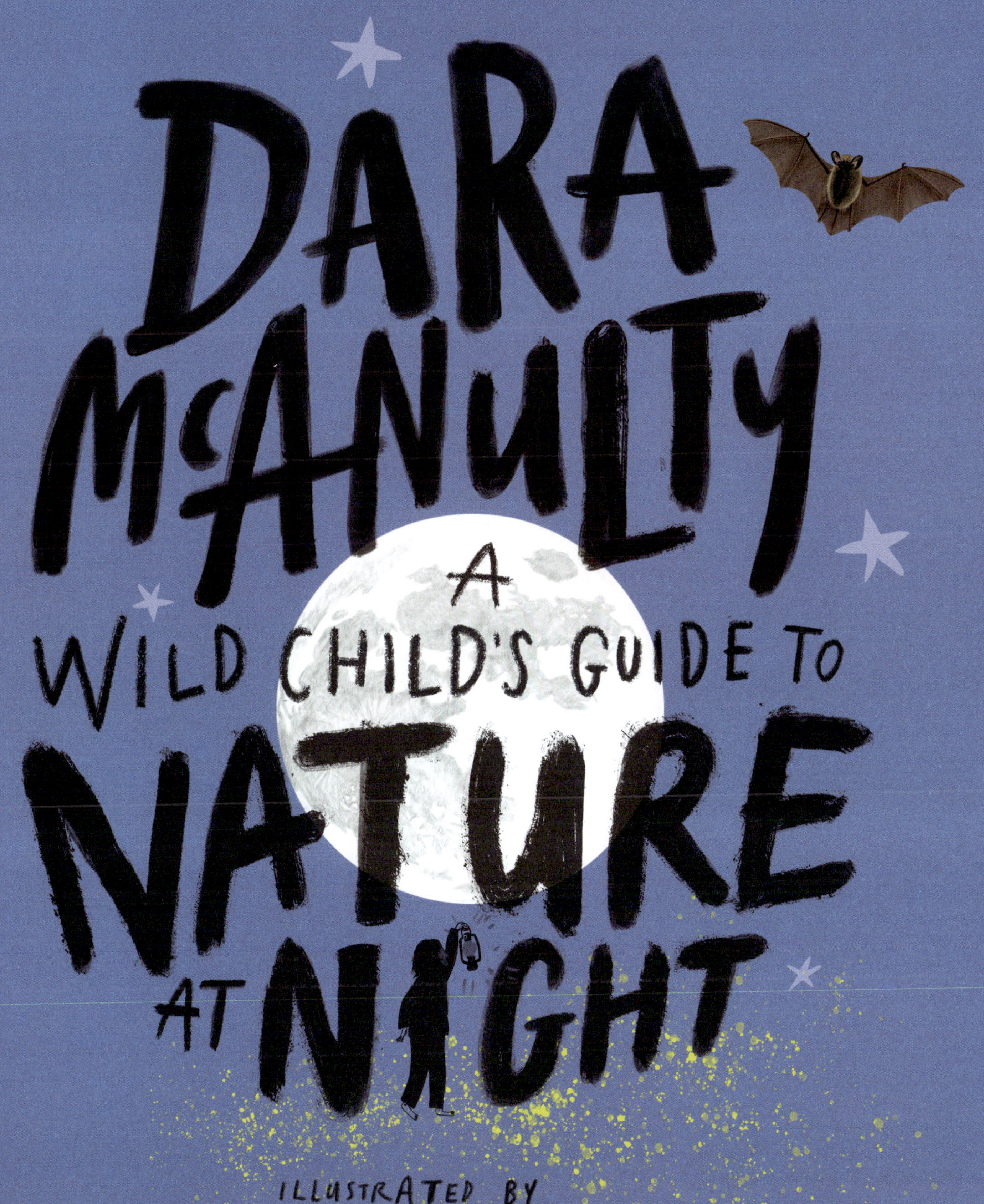

MACMILLAN CHILDREN'S BOOKS

Published 2025 by Macmillan Children's Books,
an imprint of Pan Macmillan
The Smithson, 6 Briset Street, London EC1M 5NR
EU representative: Macmillan Publishers Ireland Ltd, 1st Floor,
The Liffey Trust Centre, 117–126 Sheriff Street Upper, Dublin 1 D01 YC43
Associated companies throughout the world

ISBN 978-1-0350-2302-8

1 3 5 7 9 8 6 4 2

A CIP catalogue record for this book is available from the British Library.

Printed and bound in China

CONTENTS

HELLO
Wild
CHILd

I know you.

We have been on a journey. Above, below and on the Earth we have discovered many miracles of nature and with strong roots, we are growing, together, formed by the daily deepening of knowledge and experience.

Now it is time to go even deeper, to let the dreaming wait and adjust our eyes to the darkness of night. To search and find using all our senses, the wonders that unfold while you sleep.

Can I take your hand? Can I show you the magic of nature at night?

Let us continue our journey. A truly wild wandering. A fascinating world awaits.

At first you might feel afraid, but we won't go far, or fast. I know though that your curiosity will make you brave. Once you feel the tickle of excitement, you'll want to go further and further. Until the world, although at its darkest, will be lit with the tingling excitement of many creatures, sights and sounds, revealing themselves.

Always remember to be gentle, that you are a protector of nature, you are a guardian and a seeker.

Can I take you on one more journey?

Your friend, a friend of nature.

Dara

GARDEN
1
2

Tonight, instead of the usual, climbing up the stairs, snuggling under the covers, soft whisperings and drifty stares. Rather than waiting for sweet sleep and fleeting forgotten worlds. There is one that exists beyond the dreaming and is very, very real. Nightly rhythms go unnoticed, shaded beyond walls and doors. Let's illuminate it all now and open a portal of wonder, wide.

Watch for mysterious flutters, shadowy pulses and beats. Feel the flickering silence around night-scented blooms. Winged, windlit, filaments uncovered by unreal moonbeams.

The slow ambling and snuffles of a trundling sphere of spines. Gobbling and munching all that slithers, slides and creeps. Nose firmly mapping the ground, for a safe place to sleep.

Straggly legs are crawling from crevices and cracks. Weaving, softly spinning, silky filigree threads. A gosssamer artifice of lacework, you lie in wait patiently. Ready for your prey.

Can you see the gleaming, silvery paths, left by the travelling slitherer? The garden wanderer carries all, humped upon their back, and if you lift it up and move it, it will always find its way back!

Are you ready to feel the world now, its peculiar nightly displays? Let us wrap up warm for our adventure and set your senses ablaze. There are many concealed treasures to hear, feel and see.

GARDEN SPIDER
SPIDERS are some of the most fascinating creatures in the garden. The garden cross-orb weaver spider spins a powerful web to catch its prey. It wraps food into little parcels with sticky silk to preserve it for later.
These spiders spin new and intricate webs every night, eating them up in the evening to replenish their silk supply! Spider's webs are woven with strands of silk that are sticky, stretchy and remarkably strong. They are one of the most stunning creations in nature. Watch them sparkle and shimmer on a cold morning and gape in wonder! Female orb spiders are twice the size of males, both have the characteristic cross shape on their abdomen.
FACTS
HEDGEHOGS are mammals just like you and me! They have 5–7,000 spines on their body which are made from keratin – which also makes human hair and nails.
They may have very poor eyesight but they have excellent hearing and an incredible sense of smell. Hedgehogs can do it all – they can run, climb and swim!
HEDGEHOG

GARDEN SNAILS (and slugs) are gastropods – which means 'stomach with a foot' in Latin. Snails are some of the world's slowest animals, often taking more than an hour to cover just one metre. The silvery path left by snails is actually a trail of mucus which helps the snail move and climb along the surface of plants, grass and ground. Snails feed on living, dead and decaying plants and fungi, making them an integral part of the garden ecosystem and the food web.

Moth

MOTHS are an extraordinarily beautiful and diverse group of insects. There are over 2,500 species of moth in the UK and Ireland. They are important pollinators and are an essential part of the food chain, providing food for bats, amphibians and hedgehogs.

My favourite is not one of the bigger and more colourful moths, but is the silver Y moth, I once encountered over fifty at once fluttering around our buddleja bush late one summer evening. It is one of the most magical experiences I've had.

A scientist who studies moths (and butterflies) is called a lepidopterist.

INTERESTING PHENOMENA

CIRCADIAN RHYTHMS

THE INTERNAL BIOLOGICAL ALARM CLOCK OF LIVING ORGANISMS

CIRCADIAN is borrowed from Latin and translates to 'around a day' – *circa* meaning 'round' and *dies* meaning 'day'. The circadian rhythm is an internal biological alarm clock and, for almost all living things, it happens within a twenty-three to twenty-seven-hour period. It controls most creatures' daily schedules from when we eat and sleep to when flowers will open and close their petals. Our circadian rhythms regulate our behaviour so that we do the right activity at the right time. Circadian rhythms respond to light and darkness in the environment. You may sleep at night but there are many animals who live in a directly opposite way!

WHY ARE MANY ANIMALS NOCTURNAL?

As life became more diverse over millions of years, creatures looked for new spaces to exist and thrive. While humans rise with the light of the Sun, many animals wake when the light fades and darkness settles. Humans are diurnal, meaning active in the day, but animals which have a night-time alarm clock are called nocturnal (from Latin *nocturnalis*, meaning belonging to the night). Nocturnal animals have evolved brilliant adaptations which help them to survive in darkness.

SENSATIONAL SENSES

Some animals like the fennec fox escape the intense heat of the desert by hunting in the cool of the night. Many of the animals you meet in this book rely on the night to hunt, mate and avoid predators. They have special senses to help.

EXCEPTIONAL EYESIGHT

Many nocturnal animals such as foxes, deer and deep-sea fish have exceptional eyesight, assisted by a special reflective surface at the back of each eye. Called the tapetum lucidum, this surface works like a mirror to reflect light as it passes through the eyeball. The eye can then absorb more light, even in the dimness of night or deep water, allowing the animal to see better in the dark. While in the jungle in Borneo at night, I saw the effect of this brilliant adaptation as I spied dozens of glowing pairs of eyes!

HONED HEARING

Nocturnal moths have evolved amazing ear-like organs called tympanum membranes, which allows them to hear bats from thirty metres away. When bats are detected, moths spiral hectically through the air to dodge being gobbled up!

Owls have asymmetric ears – one ear is higher than the other – so as to triangulate and pick up sounds from all directions.

HOW CAN WE CREATE A HAVEN FOR NOCTURNAL WILDLIFE IN OUR GARDENS?

DON'T BE TOO TIDY!

Have a leaf pile. Decaying plants create habitats: they provide safe spaces and food sources for many different creatures, from insects to mammals. Hedgehogs love to snuggle down in deep leaf piles to hibernate during the winter.

Create a log pile village. Even a small pile of sticks will provide shelter and food. You can pile dead wood from your garden or from a local tree surgeon (never take dead wood from nature as that is already providing a safe space for nature) in a shady spot where fungi and moss can grow, and insects and nocturnal creatures can enjoy the store of delights.

Don't strim your garden in autumn and winter: a hedgehog could be hibernating under shrubs!

PLANTING FOR NOCTURNAL WILDLIFE

Moths and other nocturnal, flying pollinators love to feed on the pollen of honeysuckle, jasmine, phlox and evening-primrose. These plants have all evolved to attract moths and so release their scent at night. Keeping an area of long grass is great for biodiversity. Think of all the many creatures that it provides a home for during the day and the night. Beetles, crickets, grasshoppers, spiders, shrews and frogs. Often, when we leave an area of grass to grow wild, we discover wildflowers also grow too – a double win!

DIM THE LIGHTS

Using artificial lighting at night-time, especially during dawn and dusk, interferes with and disrupts the habits and circadian rhythms of nocturnal wildlife, including navigation, migration and plant blooming. This is a wider problem but we can all help if we dim the lights in our gardens.

CONNECT YOUR GARDEN TO OTHER GARDENS

If you have a garden surrounded by a fence, you can make a small opening to allow hedgehogs and other wildlife to travel the distances they need to find food and shelter. Hedgehogs love to travel. A 'wildlife corridor' allows free movement of wildlife throughout the most important urban wildlife habitat – our very own garden!

As the last velvet wing of roosting crows tucks tight, goodnight cawing chatters softly subside. Other wings unfurl readying to glide, to soar soundlessly across a darkening, inky, indigo sky. Sleeping gives way to waking for the creatures of the forest, a darkly wooded treasure, waiting to be uncovered. As lively as in daylight but observed in a different way.

Along the woodland edge from intricate underground passages, monochrome faces emerge, sniffing the moonlit air. Gathering as a family, to forage, frolic and play, their care so tender, bonds so strong.

Two are calling stoutly, quavering to and fro, tirelessly defending their domain, their home. Chestnut feathers silent, pouncing unannounced, claw upon dazzled prey: scoop and up!

Glittering eyes reflecting as a shadowy figure transpires. A slinking shape now darting, like a phantom between dimness and light. Leaving a longing, an imagining of a flicking snow-capped tail.

Pirouetting and tumbling as leaves are thrown by wind. Delicate origami wings, scattered shapes take form. Speedy shadows flitting fast, in and out of sight, dervishes, sorcerers, majesties of twilight.

Moving through the darkness, our senses pricked, alert. Excitement building stealthily, catching our foggy breath. The night is full of magnificence, joyous inner light to feel, we'll continue exploring now, see what other gifts are revealed.

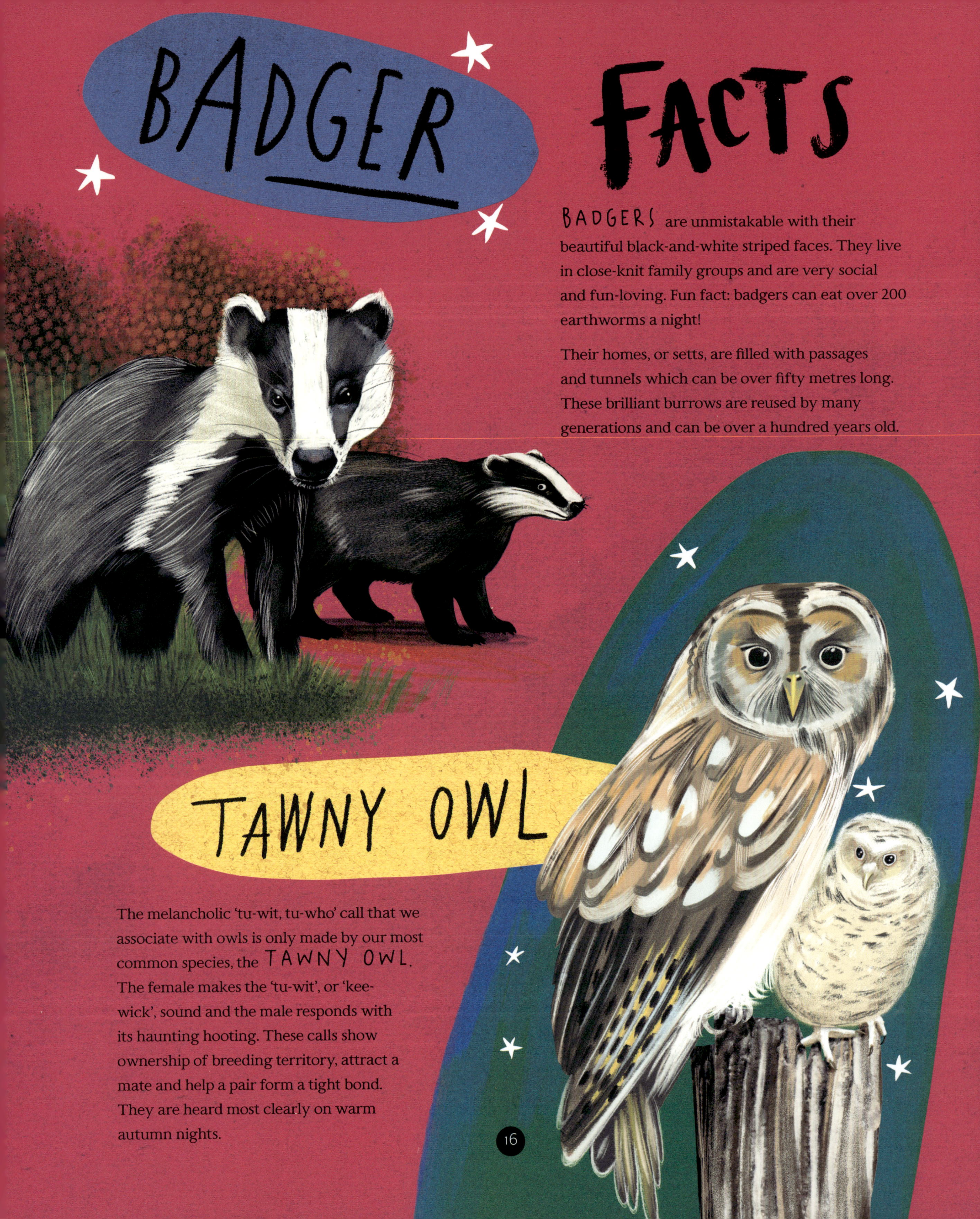

BADGER FACTS

BADGERS are unmistakable with their beautiful black-and-white striped faces. They live in close-knit family groups and are very social and fun-loving. Fun fact: badgers can eat over 200 earthworms a night!

Their homes, or setts, are filled with passages and tunnels which can be over fifty metres long. These brilliant burrows are reused by many generations and can be over a hundred years old.

TAWNY OWL

The melancholic 'tu-wit, tu-who' call that we associate with owls is only made by our most common species, the TAWNY OWL. The female makes the 'tu-wit', or 'kee-wick', sound and the male responds with its haunting hooting. These calls show ownership of breeding territory, attract a mate and help a pair form a tight bond. They are heard most clearly on warm autumn nights.

FOX

FOXES have fabulous hearing, especially at low frequencies – they can hear a beetle moving thirty metres away and can even detect rodents digging underground.

Foxes are speedy racers and can run up to 48 kilometres per hour. They are also great communicators, using over forty different sounds to call and chat to each other. Foxes are also extremely common in urban areas, listen out for their weird and wonderful nightly calls during the winter months.

BAT

Brilliant BATS are the only mammal with the power of flight! Most of the world's bats eat insects or fruit and our most common bat, the teeny-tiny common pipistrelle, can eat up to 3,000 midges every night, making our camping holidays and evenings in the garden much more enjoyable. The Daubenton's bat feeds above the surface of water, scooping up insects as it goes.

NATURE'S SONAR SYSTEM

ECHOLOCATION

Bats and toothed whales have a very special set of navigation and hunting skills. They see with sound to detect objects and gain more information about the object's distance, texture and size in complete darkness. Echolocation even allows them to figure out the direction that the prey is moving in. Nature is so clever!

Dolphins, porpoises, sperm whales, orcas and pilot whales use echolocation like a map in the murky sea depths: to communicate, find their prey and navigate. All these cetaceans produce a variety of high frequency clicking sounds and send them through the water; the sounds bounce off objects and echo back to them. Sound travels five times faster in water so these fabulous marine mammals can quickly identify what prey is in the sea around them, even when the water is muddy, murky or dark. These whales and dolphins are finding it increasingly more difficult to use echolocation due to noise pollution caused by intense boat activity, military exercises and oil drilling.

Bats are expert echolocators. As insects move super-fast, bats have to outwit them. Like those of echolocating whales and dolphins, bats' calls are ultrasonic. This means they are too high-pitched for humans to hear. When bats fly through woods in the dark, they are in danger of bumping into trees, so they emit even higher frequency calls to help them navigate their way around safely. They won't fly very close to humans either. We can use a bat detector to pick up these sounds. Different bat species use different frequencies to hunt and gain information about their prey. When bats get close to their prey, the calls increase to over 190 calls per second. It's so fun and interesting to listen to these diverse calls on a bat detector.

Pygmy shrews use a basic form of echolocation to detect the world around them. They use tittery calls, which gives them information about their habitat. Their extremely poor eyesight means they rely on these high-pitched calls to guide their way underground. Extra fun facts: pygmy shrews use tiny little beetle burrows for their homes, and no two pygmy shrews sound the same – their calls are unique!

PEOPLE POWER!

MIGHTY HUMANS HELPING WILDLIFE TO THRIVE

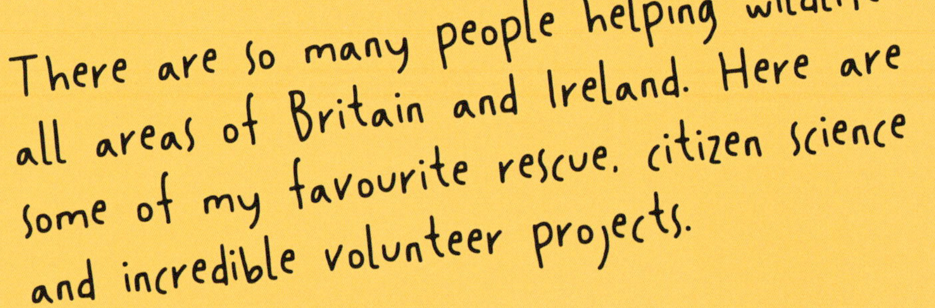

There are so many people helping wildlife in all areas of Britain and Ireland. Here are some of my favourite rescue, citizen science and incredible volunteer projects.

TIGGYWINKLES WILDLIFE HOSPITAL FOUNDATION

I first came across the wonderful Tiggywinkles Wildlife Hospital when I was researching hedgehogs as a primary school child – just like you! I was captivated by their brilliant and tireless work. It is one of the busiest and most advanced wildlife hospitals in the world and in its forty-seven years has treated over 300,000 animals! In 1978 Sue and Les Stocker and their son, Colin, began to take in injured wildlife, which they treated in their own home. Soon, everyone far and wide brought casualties to their door. In 1984 they raised a massive awareness campaign for hedgehogs as a record number were admitted to the hospital in that year.

Tiggywinkles have returned so many animals to the wild. Even though hedghehog numbers are at an all-time low, they provide a safe haven and are doing great work to save the species. Many volunteers give their time and effort to support and care for wildlife at Tiggywinkles. Amazing work!

VOLUNTEER BATWORKERS AND THE BAT CONSERVATION TRUST

I have helped my dad look after many injured bats and nursed them back to health. Seeing him hold one of these beautiful creatures in his hand and feeding it mealworms – pure magic! My dad is just one of hundreds of volunteers all around the UK who care for bats in many different ways. You need special training and a licence to rehabilitate bats like my dad does.

Volunteers also help with bat surveys, counting bats to help ecologists estimate numbers and species health, or volunteer with the National Bat Helpline, talking to people who have found an injured bat or who are worried for bats in general. The Bat Conservation Trust works very hard to make the public aware of the importance of bats. We can make our gardens more bat friendly. Having a small pond is one of the best things we can do as ponds create a habitat for midges – bats' favourite food!

TOADS ON ROADS

Toads on Roads is a fantastic and necessary project, managed by the charity Froglife. It aims to literally help toads cross roads! Toads love to migrate through the same routes over and over again, generation to generation, trying to get to their breeding grounds, and modern life has been getting in the way more and more. Roads cutting across migration routes cause huge numbers of toads to die on the roads. Hundreds of volunteers all over the United Kingdom, including children and families, visit regular migratory paths in the dead of night, in all weathers during the late winter months, to help toads to safety. What a way to help wildlife! In 2024, Toad Patrols helped 134,532 toads at 247 toad-crossing points. Wow!

BADGER TRUST and BADGER SCOTLAND

The Badger Trust is an amazing charity helping our beautiful badgers. They have over fifty connected groups full of volunteers helping badgers to thrive in an ever-changing world. Volunteers monitor and survey badger setts to make sure the badger clan is safe and well. This a brilliant opportunity to view badgers in a safe environment! They also rescue and rehabilitate injured or orphaned badgers. Badger Scotland, alongside the Scottish Wildlife Trust, have a brilliant project called 'Earn Your Stripes' helping young people learn about conservation, connect with nature and enable them to really care for and protect our wildlife.

3

COUNTRYSIDE

Passing through the edge lands, canopied skies open wide, revealing stitched-together greens, bordered by fence or hedge. Spaced out houses, silent machines, lit windows banishing, indigo inky darkness. At first the silence, breathtaking, tugging our hammering hearts, but suddenly reverberating callings, important stories to tell.

Oh, the crex, the crex is calling, a perpetual nightly lament, relentless rasping rattles, meadow shivers in regret. Its body in clever camouflage, neck craned to the Moon, when will he find his mate? Never, sometime, soon?

Hawthorn hedgerow quivers, a miniscule visitor rummages. Wide-eyed, timid and agile, a golden elusive scuttling. Nibbling, carving hazelnuts, munching bramble petals, and later, blushing berries.

A sparkling army is marching to a collective, invisible beat, migrating to ancient breeding grounds, cradled by human hands. Arriving at the glistening pond to pompously out-croak, a valiant cacophonous chorus, all for an embracing bond.

The water architects are busy. Gnawing, coppicing trees. Sculpting the riverbank, making homes for many to live. Paddling upstream gracefully, transporting with steadfast care, building blocks for nature, to thrive and for us to care.

Such a wonderful world we live in and share with splendid beings; fascination, enchantment, disbelief, learning! We must weave our threads together, with every living thing and show our full compassion, even if they do not sing.

The teeny-tiny HAZEL DORMOUSE (they weigh around 20 grams!) is one of our rarest and most endangered mammals, only found in woodlands and hedgerows in the south of England and a few areas in the Lake District and Wales. They are an arboreal species, which means they spend most of their time up trees. Dormice are marvellous acrobats, when they are not sleeping (which they do, a lot) they are scrambling along the branches of trees, grabbing on with their specially shaped paws. Dormice population has declined rapidly due to hedgerows being cut too short and too often.

CORNCRAKES belong to the rail family, along with coots and moorhens. Unlike them, corncrakes are highly active at night. They love the tall grasses of meadows and fields. They were once so abundant everywhere in the UK and Ireland, that many older people have memories of their haunting rasp all through the night. Their decline is mostly due to the intensive way in which we farm the land. Where once we had people cutting the grass with scythes, now we have large machinery, so corncrake nests and their young don't have a chance. I was so very lucky to hear a corncrake calling on Rathlin Island, one warm and balmy summer evening. It was a special, yet truly heartbreaking experience, for his call remained unanswered with no female to hear him. When nature's alarm bell sounds, we must heed its call and do all we can to raise our voices.

BEAVER

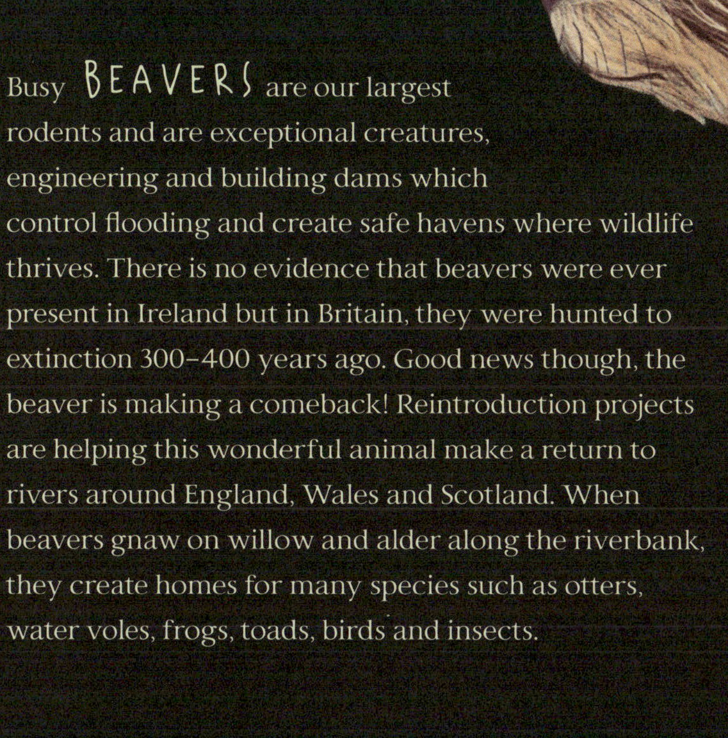

Busy BEAVERS are our largest rodents and are exceptional creatures, engineering and building dams which control flooding and create safe havens where wildlife thrives. There is no evidence that beavers were ever present in Ireland but in Britain, they were hunted to extinction 300–400 years ago. Good news though, the beaver is making a comeback! Reintroduction projects are helping this wonderful animal make a return to rivers around England, Wales and Scotland. When beavers gnaw on willow and alder along the riverbank, they create homes for many species such as otters, water voles, frogs, toads, birds and insects.

COMMON TOAD

COMMON TOADS are often spotted around Britain, but not in Ireland. Natterjack toads are much rarer, but they are found in County Kerry, in Ireland. Most toads have dry, bumpy skin that is olive or brown in colour. Special body parts called parotid glands secrete powerful toxins from a toad's skin, letting predators swiftly realize that these amphibians are not very good to eat! Toadlets hatch from pearly strings of toadspawn, unlike the globular clumps of frogspawn. Common toads have a strong migratory instinct, and, on some spring nights, thousands of them gather at ponds and lakes to find a mate and breed.

WHAT DO ANIMALS DO IN THE DARK & COLD OF WINTER?

BADGERS

As the air gets colder and school mornings and early evenings are shrouded in darkness, many creatures begin to slow down to save energy. It is a profound evolutionary act of survival.

Badgers eat lots of food in autumn and retreat underground between November and February. They don't fully hibernate, but they go into a state of torpor, which means they sleep very deeply, during cold and snowy periods. They bring in extra bedding to wrap themselves up nice and warm. They shelter as a family and love to be as comfortable as possible. When resting, badgers use up the fat reserves they have built up during autumn, but they may wake during milder days to forage and feed, before sleeping once more.

Some of our butterflies spend the winter as a chrysalis – a still, dormant phase. Some (red admiral, small tortoiseshell, comma, brimstone and peacock) overwinter as adults, sometimes inside our houses, but can be rudely awakenend when we turn the heating on at its highest. This can cause a lot of problems as weather conditions are appalling and there is little food. If you find a sleeping butterfly, you could gently move it to a colder place such as a garage or shed.

HIBERNATION

Bats, hedgehogs and dormice truly hibernate and are the only native mammals to do so. Hibernation is deeply mysterious. It's not just about sleeping, but conserving energy when conditions are harsh and food is scarce! Hibernating animals experience immense changes in their bodily functions. As the temperature drops lower and lower, their breathing slows and their heart rates drop dramatically.

A bat's heart rate can fall from 400 to 11 beats per minute. A hedgehog usually takes around twenty-five breaths a minute. During hibernation they can stop breathing, holding their breath from several minutes to two hours, before breathing rapidly for up to thirty minutes. Hazel dormice spend three quarters of the year asleep but truly hibernate between October and April. They weave little nests from hay and leaves right on the ground and curl up in a ball with their tail tucked in tight.

WAYS TO SEE NATURE AT NIGHT

SAND TRAP

Capture wildlife tracks with a sand trap in your garden

YOU WILL NEED:

A shallow baking tray

Playsand – such as the sand for a sandpit

Water

Long ruler

Small dish/bowl

Meat-based cat or dog food

1 Fill the baking tray with sand and mix in a little water to make the sand stickier (we want to see the wildlife prints).

2 Smooth the surface with a ruler and check that the trap works by pressing your finger in the sand. It should leave an indent, you can smooth this over with your ruler.

3 Place the dish with food in the middle of the tray and leave the tray overnight.

4 Check your trap and find out who has been visiting your garden!

MOTH TRAPS

You can attract magnificent moths to your garden in a really simple way! All you need is a large white sheet and a bright torch. Make sure all the lights inside and outside your house are off first. Patience is key here, so make sure you are comfortable and warm. Observing the natural world closely makes you attuned to being still and aware. These are such wonderful skills to have!

1. Hang your white sheet over a washing line, wall or other high surface.

2. Shine your torch at its brightest, wait, watch and be amazed.

If you'd like to record what you see, have your notebook to hand. Remember though, it's not necessary, you can just 'be' in the moment, have fun and feel the wonder.

If you have your notebook, count the number of moths that you spot. Record the temperature, weather, time of day and the season. When you see a moth, note down its colour, shape and size. Does it have any distinctive features?

This will help you identify what kind of moth it is.
If you get the 'mothing' bug, there are specialist 'traps' you can buy which painlessly contain the moths in a tray overnight so you can closely identify and study them. I have been on many moth-trapping adventures, they are phenomenally fun. You need to get up very early though, the moths need to fly free as soon as possible after sunrise.

EYESHINE

If you take a torch into your garden or out with you on your night-time walk, try this cool trick . . .

Place the torch between your eyes on your forehead on full beam, and animals with a reflective tapetum lucidum will shine right back at you. You will see tiny dots of light darting around your garden. This is a very neat way of seeing how biodiverse your garden is.

4

HEATH

Let us step away from the embrace of trees and feel the wide expanse. Your feet bounce on tussocks soft, heather scents the luminous path. Hold my hand tightly, as Moon lures us on; towards shining orbs, strange sounds, moving shadows, purring growls.

LAND

But wait! There is a rustling in the undergrowth, can you hear the gurgles and squeaks? An acrobat is climbing, furtively scrambling with ease. A blink of white, twinkling eyes, it's time to really leave the woods behind!

As we enter a living dreamworld, we can't believe our eyes. Pearly starlight above us, jade glowing as we rise. Tiny wriggling pulses, quietly perched in wait. Crouching to get closer, hands sparkle, heart buckles, in awe.

Rhythmic mechanical whirrings, from where, it's impossible to tell. Until churring gives way to wingbeat, ascending to clapping flight. Fern owl shadow flits and flicks, jittering, before it stills and disappears.

Golden ears appear on the hill crest. Moonlight catches watching guards. Standing to attention quickening in quivering, electric arcs. Springing bounds, leaping low, leaving tremoring space, where did it go?

I can see your eyes are drooping, even though your smile is wide. The golden hare our beacon, that it is finally dreaming time. Warmth and softness are close, but I see excitement still bubbling. Sleepy fables in starry patterns a perfect lullaby to wind wild child down.

FACTS

PINE MARTEN

PINE MARTENS are very elusive nocturnal mammals, similar in size to a domestic cat. Sometimes though, like many nocturnal animals, they are active with the summer evening light. They prefer woodland, but in some places they have spread out into heathland, especially in Scotland. They forage for fruit, fungi, insects, small rodents and birds' eggs. They are very shy and hard to spot but I have seen them on the final phase of a walk, when we are all tired and quiet. A snapshot of an unmistakable form following a rustling. They are a joy to spot.

Pine martens are rare. They have been persecuted for visiting farms and houses, which they do so because of habitat loss and when food is scarce. They are a beautiful and protected animal, essential to the ecosystem of the British Isles.

GLOW-WORM

GLOW-WORMS are known as 'Lanterns of the Heath', but did you know that they are not actually worms and not all glow-worms glow?

Believe it or not, glow-worms are small beetles and live up to three years as predatory larvae, living under rocks and hidden in heather. They only live as adults for a few weeks, maturing and producing young during the warmth of summer.

Adult male glow-worms develop wings, giving them the ability to fly and find their mating partner – but they do not glow! Only the adult female, who has remained flightless and nocturnal, glows.

NIGHTJAR

NIGHTJARS are summer migrants, visiting our heathlands from the scrub grasslands of the Democratic Republic of Congo. They have gorgeously tapered wings and are similar to the shape of a kestrel in flight. They are wizards of camouflage: their cleverly cryptic plumage resembles logs and leaves and allows them to hide in the shady undergrowth or inconspicuously perch horizontally on the branch of a tree, as still as a twig.

They are insectivores, feeding on a wide range of moths, flies and beetles. They emerge as darkness falls from their resting spots into the wide heathland skies, their whirring wing-claps filling the air with eerie, evocative sounds.

MOUNTAIN HARE

Iconic MOUNTAIN HARES live in heights above 300 metres – they are timid and easily frightened by humans and predators. Hares will only become active in daylight when moving fearfully quickly, running at 60 kilometres per hour. Hares don't live in burrows as rabbits do, but hunker low in the heather and grass.

Their beautiful fur blends wonderfully with the seasons. They moult their grey-brown coat in early winter, turning the colour of the brightest upland snow and in late spring they moult again more to mimic the colours of the moorland. Mountain hares gather together at dusk to graze, though in the day they rest alone. Their hind feet are heavily furred during winter, acting like snowshoes to help distribute their weight evenly so they don't sink into the depths – such a clever adaptation!

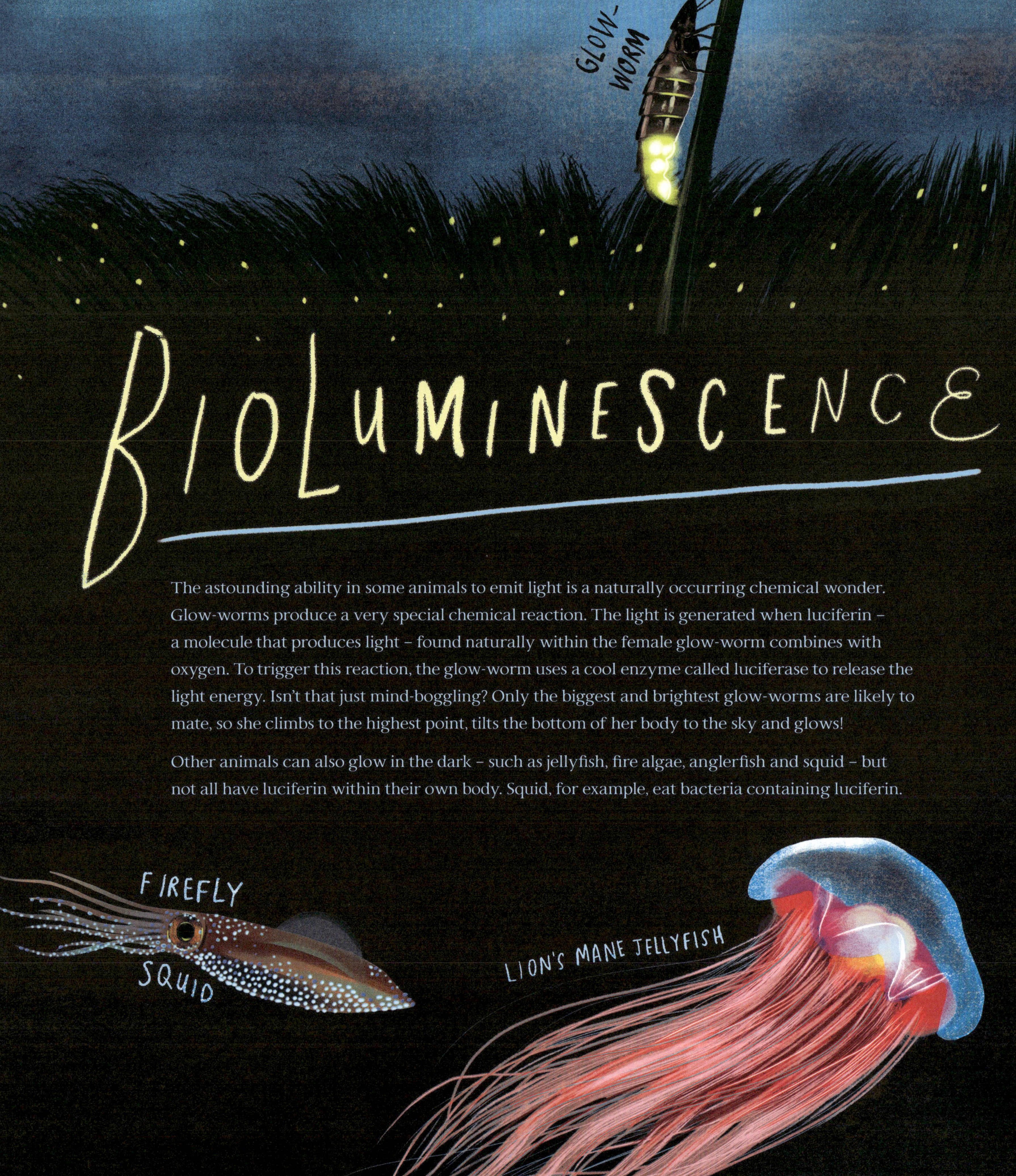

BIOLUMINESCENCE

The astounding ability in some animals to emit light is a naturally occurring chemical wonder. Glow-worms produce a very special chemical reaction. The light is generated when luciferin – a molecule that produces light – found naturally within the female glow-worm combines with oxygen. To trigger this reaction, the glow-worm uses a cool enzyme called luciferase to release the light energy. Isn't that just mind-boggling? Only the biggest and brightest glow-worms are likely to mate, so she climbs to the highest point, tilts the bottom of her body to the sky and glows!

Other animals can also glow in the dark – such as jellyfish, fire algae, anglerfish and squid – but not all have luciferin within their own body. Squid, for example, eat bacteria containing luciferin.

WHAT IS AN ATOM?

An atom is the basic building block of all matter.

WHAT IS A MOLECULE?

A molecule is a group of two or more atoms that bond together.

WHAT IS A CHEMICAL REACTION?

A chemical reaction is the process by which we can construct or deconstruct molecules, sometimes with flashes of light, explosions or temperature changes as energy is added or taken away.

WHAT IS AN ENZYME?

Enzymes are molecules and proteins that speed up chemical reactions in living things.

WHOSE SCAT IS THAT?

All elements of the natural world are fascinating and special, and this includes animal poo! I have spent many an hour searching for traces left by wildlife and learning about what different animals eat – using the best evidence there is! Never touch animal poo without proper supervision from experts though, as it contains harmful bacteria. You can note the size, shape, colour and use a stick to poke around in it instead!

FOX

FOX poo is very similar to that of a dog: it is smelly and has a twist or point at the end. It is filled with fur, feathers, teeny bones, seeds and berries. Foxes which live in urban areas have lighter-coloured poo because they are eating human food waste rather than their usual, wild diet.

PINE MARTEN poo is very noticeable and identifiable, once you know what you are looking for. It is usually dark in colour and shaped like a continuous squiggle, a bit like a coiled sausage! Pine martens intentionally leave their scat in prominent positions such as atop walls or rocks to mark their territory. In late summer it can be cherry red in colour due to their love of rowan and bilberries.

BADGER

All members of a BADGER group poo in the same shallow pit or latrine, a short distance away from their sett. These poo pits mark the territory boundaries of each badger clan. Their poo is very dark and firm but if they have been eating lots of worms, their poo will be much slimier, if berries are on the menu, expect purple poo, and always expect it to be especially pongy!

HARE

HARE droppings are pebble-shaped, much bigger than those of a rabbit and lighter in colour. They contain larger plant matter such as roots, herbs and fungi. Hares and rabbits eat their own droppings soon after they poo! This is called refection and it allows the animals to obtain more nutrients from their food – especially useful as grass is very hard to digest.

HEDGEHOG

Finding a HEDGEHOG dropping in your garden is becoming far too rare, but if you are lucky enough to spot one it will be dark brown, grey or black scattered with shiny beetle wings. For healthy hedgehog poo we need to look after the land, especially by attracting beetles (a hedgehog's favourite food) to our gardens with compost heaps and log piles.

5
SKY

*What an adventure we've had, wild child,
story guides brought us here. To our safe nest, our burrow,
how wonderfully lucky we are. Let's tuck you in tight, wild child,
I'll stay and speak brave spells, of shapeshifting heroes, to astral sentinels.
Shimmering and glimmering, afar.*

*The wandering bard looked back, his trembling fear too great,
and in the depths of the underworld, sealed his tragic fate.
The oracle, a prophet, with too much knowledge to share,
flew finally free to the heavens. Look up and see him there!*

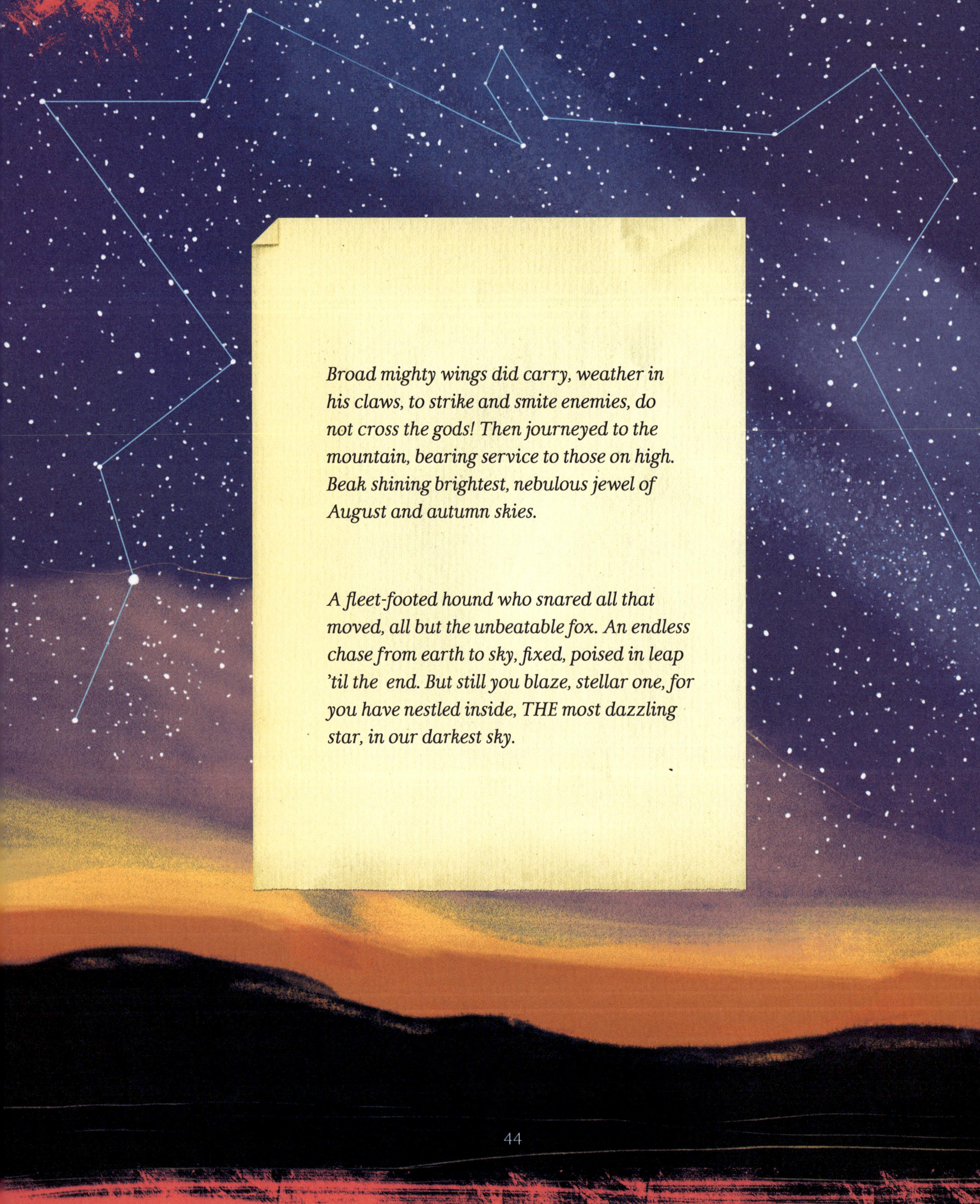

Broad mighty wings did carry, weather in his claws, to strike and smite enemies, do not cross the gods! Then journeyed to the mountain, bearing service to those on high. Beak shining brightest, nebulous jewel of August and autumn skies.

A fleet-footed hound who snared all that moved, all but the unbeatable fox. An endless chase from earth to sky, fixed, poised in leap 'til the end. But still you blaze, stellar one, for you have nestled inside, THE most dazzling star, in our darkest sky.

Trusted messenger of the gods, alerted by golden song, from the darkest depths rescued, the poet from oceans swell. Carried him to safer shores, settled on a boulder to wake, and recite to all who would listen of the cetacean, most great.

Goodnight, precious wild child, your eyelids flicker with dreams. I know you will go forth now, to love, cherish and protect. All that flutters, flicks and crawls. Soars, sweeps and sails.

Where, now?

The SKY AT NIGHT

The constellations have been used for millennia by sailors (and some animals!) to navigate their way in the dark. As a result, the constellations in our night sky are full of myths, stories and legends created as the humans below tried to make sense of the dazzling stars above them.

CYGNUS

One of the myths surrounding CYGNUS, or the swan constellation, is that of Orpheus, the wandering poet and musician featured in many different Greek legends. When his beloved wife Eurydice tragically died of a snakebite, he journeyed in to the Underworld to retrieve her. He charmed everyone he met on the way, even Hades. The King of the Underworld agreed that Eurydice could return to the land above as long as, when the pair walked out of the Underworld, neither of them looked back. As Orpheus reached the sunlight, he looked back in delight. A forbidden look, a failed mission. Eurydice was lost. Afterwards, he roamed the earth, played his lyre and sang his music. Even death could not silence him for his head still sang and began to speak powerful prophecies to those who would listen. Eventually, the God Apollo silenced him by transforming him into a swan among the stars. Alongside is his faithful lyre, represented by the constellation, Lyra.

AQUILA

AQUILA was the faithful servant eagle to Zeus, King of the Greek Gods. Aquila was a messenger between the mortal realm and that of the Gods. When Prometheus (an immortal giant) helped humans by bringing them fire, a furious Zeus ordered Aquila to attack Prometheus relentlessly. Hercules took pity on Prometheus and so shot Aquila with his his bow and arrow. As a measure of gratitude for Aquila's loyal service, Zeus placed the eagle in the sky. The constellation contains one of the brightest and closest stars in the night sky, Altair which is only seventeen light years away. Altair translates as eagle or vulture in Arabic and is the twelfth brightest star in the sky.

CANIS MAJOR

CANIS MAJOR, and its smaller neighbour, Canis Minor, were thought to be the hounds of Orion, the famed human hunter. One of the stories of Canis Major comes from the tale of the great hound Laelap, which could catch anything it hunted and the Teumessian fox, which could never be caught. The chase went on and on – an impossible puzzle – until Zeus turned them into stone, making them into two constellations: Canis Major and Canis Minor. Canis Major has the brightest star in the night sky, Sirius, also known as the Dog Star.

DELPHINUS

DELPHINUS tells the story of the poet Arion of Lesbos, the court muscian of Corinth. He travelled across Sicily and Italy making an enormous amount of money. His crew, consumed by jealousy, turned against him and threatened to kill him. For his last wish he was allowed to sing one more song. As he sang, Arion jumped off the boat and into the water. A dolphin sent by the god Apollo who was impressed by his melody took the lucky poet back to Corinth and turned the dolphin into stars.

MOONS AND TIDES

Although the Moon is quite far away its gravity can still affect the Earth through the ebb and flow of the tides. The gravity of the Moon pulls up the oceans and changes the sea in a regular pattern. There are usually two high and two low tides a day, but depending on the geography and dynamics of the shoreline this can change. Sand or shingle appears and disappears even when the Moon is not visible!

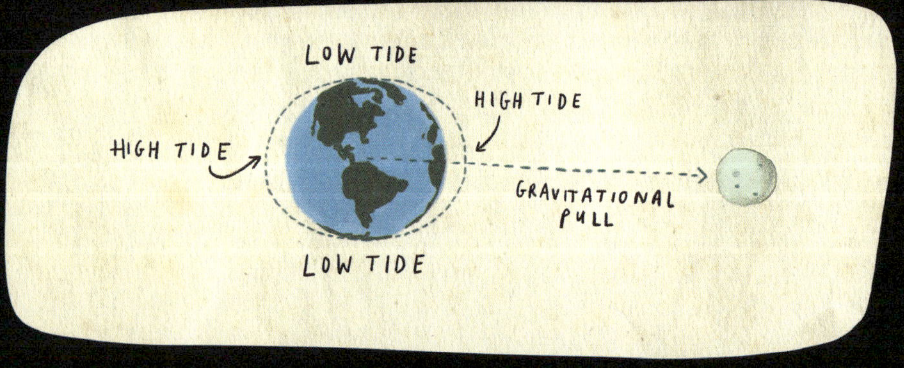

GRAVITY AND MOONQUAKES

These tidal forces also work the other way around - with the Earth pulling on the Moon. However, due to the massive size of the Earth when compared with the Moon, the tides pull and squeeze the rock of the Moon. This can cause moonquakes that can last for days.

SOLAR AND LUNAR ECLIPSES

Sometimes the orbits of the Moon, Earth and Sun line up forming a syzygy (si-zuh-jee) which can lead to us seeing a solar or lunar eclipse. The mysterious lunar eclipse occurs when the Moon is in the Earth's shadow, which prevents the Sun's light from reaching it directly. Instead, the Moon is lit up by the light that has been refracted by the Earth's atmosphere, causing the Moon to glow red. A solar eclipse occurs when the Moon gets between the Sun and the Earth, blocking out daylight. For a few minutes it becomes night as the Sun is completely blotted out.

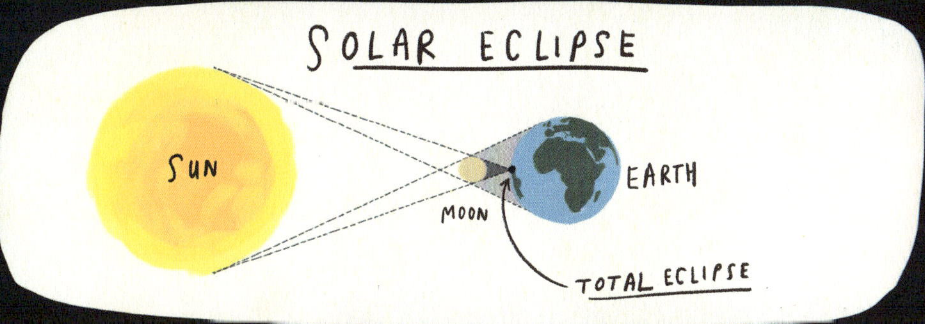

BUILD YOUR OWN CONSTELLATION PROJECTOR

YOU WILL NEED:

Thick paper

Scissors

Empty toilet paper tube

Elastic band

Toothpick

Torch (led works best) or a mobile phone

1

Trace a circle around your toilet paper tube, ensuring it is larger than the opening.

2

Cut out the circle and fasten it around one side of the tube with your elastic band. Make sure it is well secured so no light gets in!

3

With your toothpick, punch your constellation design on the paper. You can create an existing design or use your imagination. Make sure your design is the right way round as it will be symmetrically opposite from the other side of your paper tube!

4

Shine your torch through the opening on a wall in a darkened room and watch your constellation glow. You can create your own night sky!

It is so important to protect our night sky, both for humans and animals. You can help by turning off your outdoor lights at night. The sky is so VAST, we need everyone's help.

GOODBYE
Wild
Child

I know you.

I have seen your eyes sparkle when you see shapes, watching flickers of light, buzzing and fluttering. I have seen you pick up that feather. That pebble. That leaf. You have climbed the oak tree and seen the world from bird's eye, felt the wind of leaves.

I have held your hand, showed you the magic of nature.

You have been on a journey. A wild wandering. But this fascinating world still waits for you.

You have gone far from your window and garden. Delving further, further and further.

Always remember to be gentle, you are a protector of nature, a guardian, a seeker.

The next journey is yours. Go into the world and spread joy, wild child.

Your friend, a friend of nature.

Dara

Afterword

How do we spread joy? We become witnesses to beauty, knowledge and curiosity. When we do this, it shines from within us and people can't help but notice how, in being deeply connected to nature, we become truly connected to the world around us and so, to people, communities and the world. NATURE CONNECTS US TO OUR OWN HUMANITY. I say this a lot. It's *that* important.

My parents spread joy to me by pointing out all of the interesting birds and plants we encountered. By answering questions. Going to the library to learn more. All our walks took time, but all the best things in life are savoured, and enjoyed, slowly. I'll never forget my first bat walk. I was five years old. Holding my mum's hand and the bat detector in the other; I felt like an explorer! When the sounds broke through the little black box, my heart lifted. I had connected with a creature that could not be detected with human ears. It was magical. The darkness, the full Moon that suddenly appeared from the thin cloud and lit the lake to reveal Daubenton's bats skimming the surface of the glistening water. My joy in that moment reflected all that I encountered. It also lifted others around me. Perhaps they felt too nervous or shy to show their excitement. I never did and I have been told that this helped others to not hold back. So, YOU NEVER KNOW WHO YOU WILL IMPACT BY SHARING YOUR EXUBERANT ENERGY.

Badger watching at night, long hours of quiet patience and perseverance and then, the reward of observing such a carnival of antics. I thought I was the luckiest boy in the world. Seeing a cloud of silver Y moths congregate around a single buddleja bush in our small garden. A chorus of toads on a walk while camping. The simple act of observing the astonishing beauty of a spider's web, spun at night and revealed jewel-like on a frosty morning. Feeding our neighbourhood hedgehog cat food and just staring from behind the glass of our back door. Nose pressed tightly so I would see every nose snuffle, every spine. The moment a pine marten came into our garden so unexpectedly! My mum, watching from the window late at night, woke up the whole house to see. We couldn't believe it! When I was studying far from home, I walked in a specific way to find foxes at night so that I could tangibly touch my childhood. NATURE CAN DO THAT. PULL YOU BACK TO MEMORY AND THE LOVE OF THOSE WHO LOVE YOU.

All of these experiences have led me to a very special place, sharing my joy with you through the Wild Child books. It has been the greatest privilege, as a still young writer, to pass from my heart to yours, my passion and devotion to our beautiful world. To journey with you.

The next journey is yours. GO INTO THE WORLD AND SPREAD JOY, WILD CHILD.

Your friend, a friend of nature.

Abdomen
The part of an insect's body that contains organs used in digestion and reproduction.

Amphibian
An animal that has gills in its early life and lives in water, but later develops lungs and lives on land. Frogs, newts and toads are amphibians.

Atmosphere
The blanket of gases that surround Earth.

Biodiversity
This describes the richness, variety and abundance of biological life and how it interacts together.

Cetacean (suh-tay-shan)
These are mammals that live in the sea. Whales, dolphins and porpoises are cetaceans and, like us, need air to breathe.

Constellation
A group of stars that appear to make a pattern in the night sky.

Decaying
Something that is rotting, or decomposing, is described as decaying.

Dormant
A dormant animal is resting or inactive, as if it is in a deep sleep.

Ecosystem
A community or a collection of different species that interact with each other and their surroundings.

Environment
The surroundings in which a living thing exists.

Evolution
The way that animals and plants change over time, to survive in an ever-changing world.

Extinction
When a species of living thing is extinct, it has gone forever.

Forage
To search for food.

Fungi
Living things, such as mushrooms, moulds and toadstools, that produce spores and feed on living or dead matter.

Gravity
The amazing invisible force which pulls everything together. Gravity makes dropped things fall but also keeps our feet on the ground. It pulls the Moon around the Earth and the Earth around the Sun.

Graze
When animals munch on grass or gobble other plants.

Habitat
The place where an animal, plant or fungus lives.

Hibernation
The period of time when animals spend the winter in a dormant or resting state.

Insect
An animal that has six legs and a body that is divided into three main parts: head, thorax and abdomen, unlike spiders which have eight legs and two body parts.

Insectivore
An animal that mostly eats a diet of insects.

Keratin
A type of tough protein that is found in hair, nails, claws, beaks and feathers.

Larva
The juvenile (young) form of some animals which are usually very different from their adult form – such as tadpoles and caterpillars.

Mammal
A warm-blooded animal that has fur or hair and feeds its young with milk.

Migration
A long journey which animals undergo to find resources, such as food and water, or mates.

Moult
When animals shed their skin, hair or feathers at specific times of year or in their life cycle. This is necessary to grow or renew.

Mucus
A slimy substance made by an animal's body.

Navigation
Planning and following a route.

Nocturnal
Most active at night.

Nutrients
The chemicals in food that help living things to grow and stay healthy.

Pollen
A powdery substance made by the male part of a flower when they reproduce.

Pollinator
An animal, such as an insect, which transfers pollen between flowers.

Predator
An animal that hunts other animals to eat.

Prey
An animal that is hunted by other animals.

Rodent
Typically small mammals which have strong front teeth for gnawing, four legs and a tail. Beavers, rats, mice and squirrels are all rodents.

Scat
An animal's droppings.

Shrub
A woody plant that is smaller than a tree.

Species
A group of living things that are usually similar, and produce young with other members of the same group.

Territory
The area that an animal protects and defends from other animals.

Tide
The rise and fall of ocean water levels around the world caused by the Moon's gravitational pull as it goes around Earth.

Toxin
A poison made by a plant or animal.

HELPFUL ORGANIZATIONS

Societies for the Prevention of Cruelty to Animals

Northern Ireland www.uspca.co.uk

England and Wales www.rspca.org.uk

Scotland www.scottishspca.org

Ireland www.ispca.ie

Wildlife Conservation

Tiggywinkles Wildlife Hospital www.tiggywinkles.org.uk

Bat Conservation Trust www.bats.org.uk

Butterfly Conservation Trust www.butterfly-conservation.org/

Royal Society for the Protection of Birds www.rspb.org.uk

Canal and River Trust www.canalrivertrust.org.uk

Froglife (Toad Patrol) www.froglife.org

Irish Wildlife Trusts www.iwt.ie

Mammal Society www.mammal.org.uk

The Wildlife Trusts www.wildlifetrusts.org

World Wetland Trust www.wwt.org.uk

DARA McANULTY (BEM) is a multi-award-winning author and conservationist. He is the youngest ever winner of the Wainwright Prize for Nature Writing, the British Zoological Society award for communicating zoology and the RSPB Medal for conservation. He is a prolific campaigner, fundraiser and advocate for the natural world. He divides his time between Cambridge University and the Mourne Mountains, where he lives with his family in County Down.

BARRY FALLS grew up in rural Northern Ireland, where he spent a lot of time drawing pictures and writing stories to go with them. He is a commercial illustrator, who has received multiple awards for his work with clients such as *The New York Times*, *American Airlines* and *The Telegraph*.